Nine Fingerless Gloves and Mitts to Knit

Second Edition

by

Janis Frank

Thank you for purchasing this book. This book remains the
copyrighted property of the author, and may not be
redistributed to others for commercial or non-commercial purposes.
If you enjoyed this book, please encourage your friends to purchase
their own copy from their favourite book retailer.

Thank you for your support and respecting the hard work of this author.
The purchase of this book allows you to make and sell the
gloves, mittens or arm warmers you create.

Table of Contents

Welcome to the second edition of one of my most-loved knitting collections! Whether you have a few projects under your belt or are a seasoned knitter, this collection of nine fingerless glove and mitten patterns has something for everyone. You'll find plenty of inspiration and challenges to keep your needles moving.

Since the original release, I've made some exciting updates, including the addition of video tutorials to guide you through any tricky parts. You'll find direct links to these resources throughout the book. I've also added QR codes to make it even easier. If you're unfamiliar with QR codes, don't worry—they're super simple to use. Just grab your smartphone or tablet, open the camera, and point it at the code. A button will pop up on your screen, and with a quick tap, you'll be taken directly to the helpful webpage or video tutorial.

I'm thrilled to share these updated patterns with you. So grab your needles, settle in, and let's make something beautiful together!

Sizing

To help with the hand sizing, I've included a handy infographic (pun intended). Keep in mind, The gloves will stretch a bit as the stitches relax.

*** Please NOTE! ***

For the fingerless mitt patterns with a decorative motif on the back of the hand, I adjust the needle size to change the fit. This makes designing much easier and ensures the motif, like an owl, spider, hippo, and the like stays perfectly proportioned across all sizes. Plus, it just looks better overall.

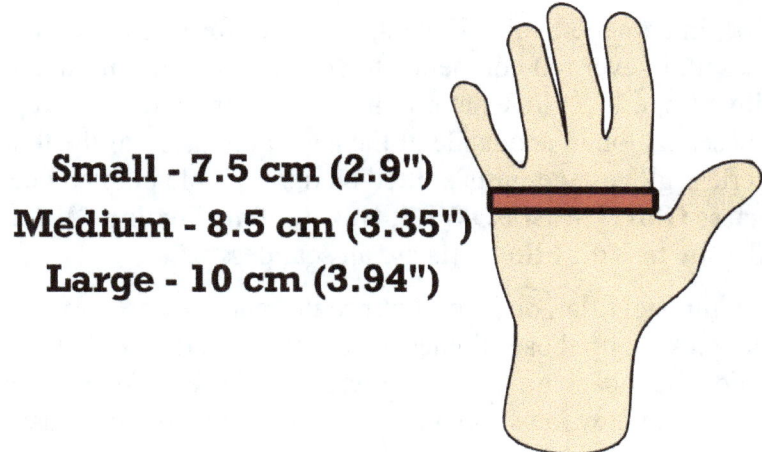

Small - 7.5 cm (2.9")
Medium - 8.5 cm (3.35")
Large - 10 cm (3.94")

Be sure to check the *Abbreviations* section specific to each pattern before you begin. I strive to keep my patterns consistent, but you may notice some differences between them. This is because a few of the patterns in this collection were written years ago, and over time, my writing style and technique abbreviations evolved.

Super Simple Fingerless Gloves

Are you just learning to knit? Tired of making dishcloths and scarves and want to make something awesome? Here is something that will make you look like a pro when it comes to knitting. A total brag-worthy design that any knitting newbie can make.

I've written a bunch of beginner patterns for slippers, but never for fingerless gloves. It was a common request, but for some reason, I never felt compelled to do so. After a bit of false starts and redesigns, I've finally come up with a fingerless glove pattern that I am happy with. I've kept the seams to a minimum and placed the seam along the outside of the hand and inside of the thumb. If you're not a fan of seams my other fingerless gloves and mitts knitted on dpn (double pointed needles) can be found in this publication. **Fingerless Gloves – with OWLS, How to Knit Texting Mittens**, **How to Knit Fingerless Gloves,** and **H**ow to Knit Flip Mitts are all seamless.

These mitts are knitted completely flat, on 2 straight needles and are perfect for the beginner. There is use of a stitch holder and picking up those stitches to complete the thumb, but it isn't difficult. Slide them on to the holder, slide them back on the needle when instructed and knit them like any other set of stitches. I have a video showing how to use a stitch holder to show you how easy it is.

I've also written the pattern to fit different sizes - small, medium and large. I use the analogy of what fits my hand. I wear a medium rubber glove and the medium size fits my hand perfectly. I wash dishes and scrub my toilets. I wear gloves when I do. If you never wear rubber or latex gloves, this won't make any sense to you, I guess. I'm only saying this because I have had complaints about my sizing references. I don't live in a gloveless kind of world but I'm glad some people do. It always amazes me what some "Karens" feel the need to complain about.

And if you need something a little more defined, the sizing guide is at the beginning of this collection. Flip back a few pages for actual measurements.

Things You Need

Worsted weight yarn

Size 6 US (4 mm) knitting needles

Stitch holder - It looks like a big safety pin

Tapestry needle

Gauge

This is important to follow for correct sizing.

2" (5 cm) = 10 sts

2" (5 cm) - 16 rows

in stockinette

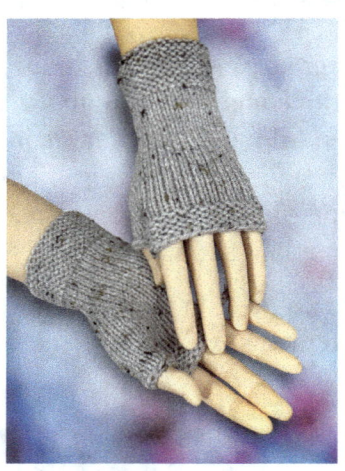

Small

Right Hand

Cast on 31

Rows 1-14: Knit across

Row 15: Knit across

Row 16: Purl across

Row 17: Knit across

Row 18: Purl across

Row 19: Knit across

Row 20: Purl across

Row 21: Knit across

Row 22: Purl across

Row 23: K18 M1 K1 M1 K12

Row 24: Purl across

Row 25: Knit across

Row 26: P12 PM1 P3 PM1 P18

Row 27: Knit across

Row 28: Purl across

Row 29: K18 M1 K5 M1 K12

Row 30: Purl across

Row 31: Knit across

Row 32: P12 PM1 P7 PM1 P18

Row 33: Knit across

Row 34: Purl across

Row 35: K18 M1 K9 M1 K12

Row 36: Purl across

Row 37: K18. Slip the next 11 stitches onto a stitch holder. K12.

Row 38: Purl across

Row 39: Knit across

Row 40: Purl across

Row 41-48: Knit across

Cast off.

Making the Thumb

Pick up the 11 stitches on the stitch holder

Row 1: Knit across

Row 2: Purl across

Row 3: Knit across

Row 4: Purl across

Cast off.

Sew seam along the side of the glove and the inside of the thumb. Work in ends.

Left Hand

Cast on 31

Rows 1-14: Knit across

Row 15: Knit across

Row 16: Purl across

Row 17: Knit across

Row 18: Purl across

Row 19: Knit across

Row 20: Purl across

Row 21: Knit across

Row 22: Purl across

Row 23: K12 M1 K1 M1 K18

Row 24: Purl across

Row 25: Knit across

Row 26: P18 PM1 P3 PM1 P12

Row 27: Knit across

Row 28: Purl across

Row 29: K12 M1 K5 M1 K18

Row 30: Purl across

Row 31: Knit across

Row 32: P18 PM1 P7 PM1 P12

Row 33: Knit across

Row 34: Purl across

Row 35: K12 M1 K9 M1 K18

Row 36: Purl across

Row 37: K12. Slip the next 11 stitches onto a stitch holder. K18.

Row 38: Purl across

Row 39: Knit across

Row 40: Purl across

Row 41-48: Knit across

Cast off.

Making the Thumb

Pick up the 11 stitches on the stitch holder

Row 1: Knit across

Row 2: Purl across

Row 3: Knit across

Row 4: Purl across

Cast off.

Sew seam along the side of the glove and the inside of the thumb. Work in ends.

Medium

Right Hand

Cast on 33

Rows 1-14: Knit across

Row 15: Knit across

Row 16: Purl across

Row 17: Knit across

Row 18: Purl across

Row 19: Knit across

Row 20: Purl across

Row 21: Knit across

Row 22: Purl across

Row 23: K19 M1 K1 M1 K13

Row 24: Purl across

Row 25: Knit across

Row 26: P13 PM1 P3 PM1 P19

Row 27: Knit across

Row 28: Purl across

Row 29: K19 M1 K5 M1 K13

Row 30: Purl across

Row 31: Knit across

Row 32: P13 PM1 P7 PM1 P19

Row 33: Knit across

Row 34: Purl across

Row 35: K19 M1 K9 M1 K13

Row 36: Purl across

Row 37: Knit across

Row 38: P13 PM1 P11 PM1 P19

Row 39: Knit across

Row 40: Purl across

Row 41: K19. Slip the next 13 stitches onto a stitch holder. K13.

Row 42: Purl across

Row 43: Knit across

Row 44: Purl across

Row 45-52: Knit across

Cast off.

Making the Thumb

Pick up the 13 stitches on the stitch holder

Row 1: Knit across

Row 2: Purl across

Row 3: Knit across

Row 4: Purl across

Cast off.

Sew seam along the side of the glove and the inside of the thumb. Work in ends.

Left Hand

Cast on 33

Rows 1-14: Knit across

Row 15: Knit across

Row 16: Purl across

Row 17: Knit across

Row 18: Purl across

Row 19: Knit across

Row 20: Purl across

Row 21: Knit across

Row 22: Purl across

Row 23: K13 M1 K1 M1 K19

Row 24: Purl across

Row 25: Knit across

Row 26: P19 PM1 P3 PM1 P13

Row 27: Knit across

Row 28: Purl across

Row 29: K13 M1 K5 M1 K19

Row 30: Purl across

Row 31: Knit across

Row 32: P19 PM1 P7 PM1 P13

Row 33: Knit across

Row 34: Purl across

Row 35: K13 M1 K9 M1 K19

Row 36: Purl across

Row 37: Knit across

Row 38: P19 PM1 P11 PM1 P13

Row 39: Knit across

Row 40: Purl across

Row 41: K13. Slip the next 13 stitches onto a stitch holder. K19.

Row 42: Purl across

Row 43: Knit across

Row 44: Purl across

Row 45-52: Knit across

Cast off.

Making the Thumb

Pick up the 13 stitches on the stitch holder

Row 1: Knit across

Row 2: Purl across

Row 3: Knit across

Row 4: Purl across

Cast off.

Sew seam along the side of the glove and the inside of the thumb. Work in ends.

Large

Right Hand

Cast on 35

Rows 1-14: Knit across

Row 15: Knit across

Row 16: Purl across

Row 17: Knit across

Row 18: Purl across

Row 19: Knit across

Row 20: Purl across

Row 21: Knit across

Row 22: Purl across

Row 23: K20 M1 K1 M1 K14

Row 24: Purl across

Row 25: Knit across

Row 26: P14 PM1 P3 PM1 P20

Row 27: Knit across

Row 28: Purl across

Row 29: K20 M1 K5 M1 K14

Row 30: Purl across

Row 31: Knit across

Row 32: P14 PM1 P7 PM1 P20

Row 33: Knit across

Row 34: Purl across

Row 35: K20 M1 K9 M1 K14

Row 36: Purl across

Row 37: Knit across

Row 38: P14 PM1 P11 PM1 P20

Row 39: Knit across

Row 40: Purl across

Row 41: K20 M1 13 M1 K14

Row 42: Purl across

Row 43: K20. Slip the next 15 stitches onto a stitch holder. K14.

Row 44: Purl across

Row 45: Knit across

Row 46: Purl across

Row 47-54: Knit across

Cast off.

Making the Thumb

Pick up the 15 stitches on the stitch holder

Row 1: Knit across

Row 2: Purl across

Row 3: Knit across

Row 4: Purl across

Cast off.

Sew seam along the side of the glove and the inside of the thumb. Work in ends.

Left Hand

Cast on 35

Rows 1-14: Knit across

Row 15: Knit across

Row 16: Purl across

Row 17: Knit across

Row 18: Purl across

Row 19: Knit across

Row 20: Purl across

Row 21: Knit across

Row 22: Purl across

Row 23: K14 M1 K1 M1 K20

Row 24: Purl across

Row 25: Knit across

Row 26: P20 PM1 P3 PM1 P14

Row 27: Knit across

Row 28: Purl across

Row 29: K14 M1 K5 M1 K20

Row 30: Purl across

Row 31: Knit across

Row 32: P20 PM1 P7 PM1 P14

Row 33: Knit across

Row 34: Purl across

Row 35: K14 M1 K9 M1 K20

Row 36: Purl across

Row 37: Knit across

Row 38: P20 PM1 P11 PM1 P14

Row 39: Knit across

Row 40: Purl across

Row 41: K14 M1 13 M1 K20

Row 42: Purl across

Row 43: K14. Slip the next 15 stitches onto a stitch holder. K20.

Row 44: Purl across

Row 45: Knit across

Row 46: Purl across

Row 47-54: Knit across

Cast off.

Making the Thumb

Pick up the 15 stitches on the stitch holder

Row 1: Knit across

Row 2: Purl across

Row 3: Knit across

Row 4: Purl across

Cast off.

Sew seam along the side of the glove and the inside of the thumb. Work in ends.

Abbreviations

K - knit

P – purl

st - stitch

sts – stitches

M1 – Make one (knit wise). Increase one stitch between the stitches. Pick up the yarn between the stitches. Twist it slightly and place it on your non-working needle. Knit the stitch. Watch this video on **How to M1 or Make 1** to see how.

PM1 – Make one (purl wise). Increase one stitch between the stitches. Pick up the yarn between the stitches. Twist it slightly and place it on your non-working needle. Purl the stitch. Watch this video on **How to PM1 or Purl Make 1** to see how.

If you need some help in how to use a stitch holder, you can watch the video **How to Use a Stitch Holder** .

Hints and Tips

Make your seams as narrow as possible when sewing them. The bulkier the seam the more noticeable and possibly uncomfortable for the wearer.

The purple fingerless mitts have 60 rows total between the garter stitch cuff and the start of the thumb gusset (Row 15 - 22). I don't think I would increase much further than that. The glove itself isn't very stretchy and won't fit further up the forearm. Too much bunching may also make the glove push its way further down and off the fingers.

I used some self-striping yarn to make these. Not all striping yarn is created equal. Some of them are designed to stripe for larger projects and don't really work for smaller projects like this. Though with saying that, you could always cut the yarn and start a new colour where you choose. You will have more ends to deal with, but I have a post that shows you **How to Work in the Ends While Knitting**. This link QR code will take you right where you need to be.

Easy to Knit Owl
Fingerless Gloves
Knit on Two Needles

Since the how-to video showing how to knit these gloves in the round went over like a lead balloon, I've put in the effort and redesigned the gloves so they can be knit flat on 2 needles. In case you still want to learn how to knit in the round or want the seamless version, you can read the pattern further along in this publication - **How to Knit Owl Fingerless Gloves**.

Like many of my knitting patterns, I've made the gloves as one pattern and adjusted the needle size to change the sizes. This makes it a heck of a lot easier to design and keeps the proportion of the owl the same on all sizes. Frankly, the overall look is better.

I've also created videos for you to see how the stitches are done, if any of them are giving you problems. I do have all the basic stitch videos on my YouTube channel. If you need any help, all of the stitches are named in the *Abbreviations* section of this pattern with QR codes linking to the videos.

Things You Need

Knitting needles:

   Small - Size 3 US (3.25 mm) knitting needles

   Medium - Size 6 US (4 mm) knitting needles

   Large - Size 8 US (5mm) knitting needles

Worsted weight yarn

Cable Needle **-** There are a number of styles but I prefer the hook version

Stitch holder – It looks like a big safety pin

Tapestry needle

Gauge

In *stockinette* stitch. This is important to have correct sizing.

Small

size 3.5 mm (US size 4) knitting needles
11 stitches every 2 inches (5 cm)
16 rows every 2 inches (5 cm)

Medium

size 4 mm (US size 6) knitting needles
10 stitches every 2 inches (5 cm)
14 rows every 2 inches (5 cm)

Large

size 5 mm (US size 8) knitting needles
9 stitches every 2 inches (5 cm)
12 rows every 2 inches (5 cm)

Left Hand

Cast on 33

Rows 1-14: Knit across

Row 15: Knit across

Row 16: Purl across

Row 17: Knit across

Row 18: Purl across

Row 19: Knit across

Row 20: P5 K1 P8 K1 P to the end of the row

Row 21: K13 M1 K1 M1 K4 P1 C4F C4B P1 K to the end of the row

Row 22: P5 K1 P8 K1 P to the end of the row

Row 23: K20 P1 K8 P1 K to the end of the row

Row 24: P5 K1 P8 K1 P4 PM1 P3 PM1 P to the end of the row

Row 25: K22 P1 K8 P1 K to the end of the row

Row 26: P5 K1 P8 K1 P to the end of the row

Row 27: K13 M1 K5 M1 K4 P1 K8 P1 K to the end of the row

Row 28: P5 K1 P8 K1 P to the end of the row

Row 29: K24 P1 C4F C4B P1 K to the end of the row

Row 30: P5 K1 P2 K4 P2 K1 P4 PM1 P7 PM1 P to the end of the row

Row 31: K26 P1 K2 P4 K2 P1 K to the end of the row

Row 32: P5 K1 P2 K4 P2 K1 P to the end of the row

Row 33: K13 M1 K9 M1 K4 P1 K2 P4 K2 P1 K to the end of the row

Row 34: P5 K1 P2 K4 P2 K1 P to the end of the row

Row 35: K28 P1 K2 P4 K2 P1 K to the end of the row

Row 36: P5 K1 P2 K4 P2 K1 P4 PM1 P11 PM1 P to the end of the row

Row 37: K30 P1 K2 P4 K2 P1 K to the end of the row

Row 38: P5 K1 P2 K4 P2 K1 P to the end of the row

Row 39: K13 Pass the next 13 sts onto a stitch holder. K4 P1 K2 P4 K2 P1 K to the end of the row

Row 40: P5 K1 P2 K4 P2 K1 P to the end of the row

Row 41: K17 P1 C4F C4B P1 K to the end of the row

Row 42: P5 K10 P to the end of the row

Row 43: Knit across

Row 44: Purl across

Row 45-50: Knit across

Cast off.

Making the Thumb

Pick up the 13 stitches on the stitch holder

Row 1: Knit across

Row 2: Purl across

Row 3: Knit across

Row 4: Purl across

Cast off.

Sew seam along the side of the glove and the inside of the thumb. Work in ends.

Right Hand

Cast on 33

Rows 1-14: Knit across

Row 15: Knit across

Row 16: Purl across

Row 17: Knit across

Row 18: Purl across

Row 19: Knit across

Row 20: P18 K1 P8 K1 P to the end of the row

Row 21: K5 P1 C4F C4B P1 K4 M1 K1 M1 K to the end of the row

Row 22: P20 K1 P8 K1 P to the end of the row

Row 23: K5 P1 K8 P1 K to the end of the row

Row 24: P13 PM1 P3 PM1 P4 K1 P8 K1 P to the end of the row

Row 25: K5 P1 K8 P1 K to the end of the row

Row 26: P22 K1 P8 K1 P to the end of the row

Row 27: K5 P1 K8 P1 K4 M1 K5 M1 K to the end of the row

Row 28: P24 K1 P8 K1 P to the end of the row

Row 29: K5 P1 C4F C4B P1 K to the end of the row

Row 30: P13 PM1 P7 PM1 P4 K1 P2 K4 P2 K1 P to the end of the row

Row 31: K5 P1 K2 P4 K2 P1 K to the end of the row

Row 32: P26 K1 P2 K4 P2 K1 P to the end of the row

Row 33: K5 P1 K2 P4 K2 P1 K4 M1 K9 M1 K to the end of the row

Row 34: P28 K1 P2 K4 P2 K1 P to the end of the row

Row 35: K5 P1 K2 P4 K2 P1 K to the end of the row

Row 36: P13 PM1 P11 PM1 P4 K1 P2 K4 P2 K1 P to the end of the row

Row 37: K5 P1 K2 P4 K2 P1 K to the end of the row

Row 38: P30 K1 P2 K4 P2 K1 P to the end of the row

Row 39: K5 P1 K2 P4 K2 P1 K4 Pass the next 13 sts onto a stitch holder. K to the end of the row

Row 40: P17 K1 P2 K4 P2 K1 P to the end of the row

Row 41: K5 P1 C4F C4B P1 K to the end of the row

Row 42: P17 K10 P to the end of the row

Row 43: Knit across

Row 44: Purl across

Row 45-50: Knit across

Cast off.

Making the Thumb

Pick up the 13 stitches on the stitch holder

Row 1: Knit across

Row 2: Purl across

Row 3: Knit across

Row 4: Purl across

Cast off.

Sew seam along the side of the glove and the inside of the thumb. Work in ends.

Hints and Tips

Make your seams as narrow as possible when sewing them. The bulkier the seam the more noticeable and possibly uncomfortable for the wearer.

You can make these gloves with a ribbed cuff and around the fingers like the original **Owl Fingerless Gloves**. You can easily do a K1 P1 ribbing to make that happen.

Abbreviation

K – knit

P – purl

st - stitch

sts – stitches

M1 – Make one (knit wise). Increase one stitch between the stitches. Pick up the yarn between the stitches. Twist it slightly and place it on your non-working needle. Knit the stitch. Watch this video on **How to M1 or Make 1** to see how.

PM1 – Make one (purl wise). Increase one stitch between the stitches. Pick up the yarn between the stitches. Twist it slightly and place it on your non-working needle. Purl the stitch. Watch this video on **How to PM1 or Purl Make 1** to see how.

Side note: I use both versions of the terminology when it comes to cable stitches. I've been corrected that I'm using the wrong one for both occasions so it's a no win for me. What I mean is that C4F is the same technique as C2F. Just like how C2B is the same as C4B. Do you think of it as the just the stitches you're pulling or the number of stitches you're using in total when you do it? It's a personal choice, I guess.

C4F - Pick up the next 2 stitches with your cable needle. Pull the stitches to the FRONT of your work. Knit the next 2 stitches on your non-working needle. Knit the 2 stitches from the cable needle. Watch this video to see how. How to C4F or Cable 4 Forward.

C4B - Pick up the next 2 stitches with your cable needle. Pull the stitches to the BACK of your work. Knit the next 2 stitches on your non-working needle. Knit the 2 stitches from the cable needle. Watch this video to see how. How to C4B or Cable 4 Back

If you need some help in how to use a stitch holder, you can watch the video **How to Use a Stitch Holder** .

How to Knit Fingerless Gloves

I'm not sure if this happens to anyone else, but I found some fantastic yarn on clearance that I absolutely had to have. Of course, I had no idea what to do with it. Then I got on my fingerless glove kick. I have written other patterns in the past such as my **Owl Fingerless Gloves**, **Flip Mitts,** and **Texting Mitts**, (all in this publication) but they were all made with standard worsted weight yarn. The yarn I couldn't leave behind was light weight; 3 as by North American terminology. So, a redesign of my gloves was in order! I absolutely love that these are a lighter, more delicate version of my previous patterns. AND I can use colour changing yarn and it works! If this is your first time using one of my patterns, I kinda got a thing for shaded yarns...just sayin'.

Like my other fingerless mitts, these are knitted on double point needles, also known as DPN. Though this sounds intimidating, it really is very simple. This is definitely not a beginner's knitting project, but knitting in the round is the same as knitting flat. Only difference is you don't flip your work back in forth; it's done a continuous circle.

The sizing for mittens, like socks or slippers, is somewhat general. The **small** size will fit someone with a smaller hand. Think a younger teenager. A **medium** is an average lady's hand. I'm a medium when it comes to rubber gloves and I designed the medium mitt to fit my hand. **Large** is for a larger size hand. Each size is written out in full as the row and stitch counts differ for each.

Things You Need

Yarn (a standard ball of light weight yarn (3 weight) will be more than enough)

Size 4 mm (US size 6) double pointed needles (or whatever size needles you need to get the correct gauge).

Stitch holder

Tapestry needle – to work in the ends

Gauge

In stockinette

11 stitches = 2 inches

17 rows = 2 inches

Small

The Mitt

Cast on 32 sts (loosely). Divide these evenly as possible on three of the double pointed needles.

Round 1 - 12: K1, P1 (Creates knit 1 purl 1 ribbing).

Round 13 - 15: Knit

Round 16: K1, M1, K1, M1, K30.

Round 17 - 18: Knit

Round 19: K1, M1, K3, M1, K30.

Round 20 - 21: Knit

Round 22: K1, M1, K5, M1, K30.

Round 23 - 24: Knit

Round 25: K1, M1, K7, M1, K30.

Round 26 - 27: Knit

Round 28: K1, M1, K9, M1, K30.

Round 29 - 30: Knit

Round 31: K1, M1, K11, M1, K30.

Round 32 - 33: Knit

Round 34: K1, place next 13 sts onto the stitch holder. K30.

Round 35 - 42: K around.

Round 43: K2tog, P1, *K1, P1* Repeat from * to * around.

Round 44 - 47: *K1, P1* Repeat from * to * around.

Bind off loosely.

The Thumb

Worked over the 13 sts on the stitch holder.

Pick up and divided the 13 sts on the stitch holder between the 3 double pointed needles. One of the needles will have more sts than the others.

Round 1 – 3: Knit

Bind off loosely.

Medium

The Mitt

Cast on 36 sts (loosely). Divide these evenly as possible on three of the double pointed needles.

Round 1 - 15: K1, P1 (Creates knit 1, purl 1 ribbing).

Round 16 - 18: Knit

Round 19: K1, M1, K1, M1, K34.

Round 20 - 21: Knit

Round 22: K1, M1, K3, M1, K34.

Round 23 - 24: Knit

Round 25: K1, M1, K5, M1, K34.

Round 26 - 27: Knit

Round 28: K1, M1, K7, M1, K34.

Round 29 - 30: Knit

Round 31: K1, M1, K9, M1, K34.

Round 32 - 33: Knit

Round 34: K1, M1, K11, M1, K34.

Round 35 - 36: Knit

Round 37: K1, M1, K13, M1,K34.

Round 38 - 39: Knit

Round 40: K1, place next 15 sts onto the stitch holder. K34.

Round 41 - 49: K around.

Round 50: K2 tog. P1, *K1, P1* Repeat from * to * around.

Round 51 - 54: *K1, P1* Repeat from * to * around.

Bind off loosely.

The Thumb

Worked over the 15 sts on the stitch holder.

Pick up and divided the 15 sts on the stitch holder between the 3 double pointed needles. One of the needles will have more sts than the others.

Round 1 – 3: Knit

Bind off loosely.

Large

The Mitt

Cast on 40 sts (loosely). Divide these evenly as possible on three of the double pointed needles.

Round 1 - 18: K1, P1 (Creates knit 1, purl 1 ribbing).

Round 19 - 20: Knit

Round 21: K1, M1, K1, M1, K38.

Round 22 - 23: Knit

Round 24: K1, M1, K3, M1, K38.

Round 25 - 26: Knit

Round 27: K1, M1, K5, M1, K38.

Round 28 - 29: Knit

Round 30: K1, M1, K7, M1, K38.

Round 31 - 32: Knit

Round 33: K1, M1, K9, M1, K38.

Round 34 - 35: Knit

Round 36: K1, M1, K11, M1, K38.

Round 37 - 38: Knit

Round 39: K1, M1, K13, M1, K38.

Round 40 - 41: Knit

Round 42: K1, M1, K15, M1,K38.

Round 43 – 44: Knit

Round 45: K1, place next 17 sts onto the stitch holder. K38.

Round 46 - 57: K around.

Round 58: K2tog, P1, *K1, P1* Repeat from * to * around.

Round 59 - 63: *K1, P1* Repeat from * to * around.

Bind off loosely.

The Thumb

Worked over the 17 sts on the stitch holder.

Pick up and divided the 17 sts on the stitch holder between the 3 double pointed needles. One of the needles will have more sts than the others.

Round 1 – 5: Knit

Bind off loosely.

Abbreviations

K – Knit

P – Purl

K2tog – knit 2 together

sts – stitches

st – stitch

M1 – Make one (knit wise). Increase one stitch between the stitches. Pick up the yarn between the stitches. Twist it slightly and place it on your non-working needle. Knit the stitch. Watch this video on **How to M1 or Make 1** to see how.

Helpful Hints

You don't need a stitch holder. Even a piece of yarn will work.

Customize this pattern as you see fit. If you want the cuff longer, do so. If you need a longer thumb, add more rows. As long as your stitch counts stay the same, it should work out fine.

Some folks like to felt their mittens as it can help stop the wind from blowing through the stitches. Be careful though because felting shrinks your work! It's hard to guess how much shrinkage will happen as there are so many variables involved, from temperature of the water to how much agitation occurs during the felting process. You can give it a try but make sure you use PURE wool! Anything that is a blend won't felt properly. My last attempt at felting a pair of mittens for myself resulted in my young son getting a new pair of mitts. At least they didn't go to waste :-/

How to Knit Fingerless Gloves with OWLS!

Also known as fingerless mittens, I seem to have a thing going on for this awesome owl motif. If you haven't seen them already, I also have a **Knitted Owl Slipper** pattern that you may like. I've also expanded to a beanie and scarf. More about that in the *More FREE Patterns* section.

But more about these awesome fingerless gloves… They are fairly quick to make if you're an experienced knitter and know how to knit in the round on double pointed needles (dpn). This is also a great pattern if you have a bit of left over yarn from other knitting projects. Like enough to knit one slipper, but you're not sure if you'll have enough to finish the whole pair. I know. We've all been there.

A few quick words on sizing. Instead of going through all the effort to remake the pattern for different sizes, and to keep the proportion of the knitted owls the same, I've gone about adjusting the sizing by changing the size of your knitting needles. These are knitted in the round making them seamless with no scratchy seams to worry about. Because of being knitted in the round, the thumbs have to be on different sides so they fit correctly. You'll have to make one for the left hand and the right hand. Instructions are given separately for both.

And as part of the latest edition of this pattern, I've created a complete how-to video showing every single round on YouTube! If you are stuck or need a little clarification, maybe this is your first time knitting in the round on DPN, this video will help you immensely. You can look for this title **How to Knit Fingerless Owl Gloves or Mitts** to watch it for free on my Youtube channel or simply take a photo of this QR code and watch the video on your phone or tablet.

Things You Need

Worsted weight yarn (less than 50 grams was more than enough to make a pair of large knitted gloves. I know because I weighed them). I used Red Heart worsted weight yarn when designing the pattern but any kind will do.

Set of 4 double pointed needles (see *Gauge* section)

Stitch holder

Needle and thread to sew on eyes

Tapestry needle to sew the hole by the thumb and work in ends

Cable needle

4 – 4 mm beads for eyes. You can use larger ones or very small buttons, too. I use some half jewels I found and glue them on.

Gauge

In *stockinette* stitch

Small

size 3.5 mm (US size 4) single pointed needles
11 stitches every 2 inches (5 cm)
16 rows every 2 inches (5 cm)

Medium

size 4 mm (US size 6) single pointed needles
10 stitches every 2 inches (5 cm)
14 rows every 2 inches (5 cm)

Large

size 5 mm (US size 8) single pointed needles
9 stitches every 2 inches (5 cm)
12 rows every 2 inches (5 cm)

Left Hand

Cast on 36 sts **loosely** (you need to allow the ribbing to stretch)

Round 1 – 10: K1 P1

Round 11 – 13: K around

Round 14: K1 M1 K1 M1 K6 P1 K8 P1 K18 (knitted stitches between the M1's are the thumb increase)

Round 15: K around to the P. P1C4F C4B P1 K18

Round 16: K around to the P. P1 K8 P1 K18

Round 17: K1 M1 K3 M1 K6 P1 K8 P1 K18

Round 18: Repeat round 16

Round 19: Repeat round 16

Round 20: K1 M1 K5 M1 K6 P1 K8 P1 K18

Round 21: Repeat round 16

Round 22: Repeat round 16

Round 23: K1 M1 K7 M1 K6 P1 C4F C4B P1 K18

Round 24: K around to the P. P1 K2 P4 K2 P1 K18

Round 25: Repeat round 24

Round 26: K1 M1 K9 M1 K6 P1 K2 P4 K2 P1 K18

Round 27: Repeat round 24

Round 28: Repeat round 24

Round 29: K1 M1 K11 M1 K6 P1 K2 P4 K2 P1 K18

Round 30: Repeat round 24

Round 31: Repeat round 24

Round 32: K1 Pass the 13 stitches to the stitch holder (the thumb stitches). K to the P. P1 K2 P4 K2 P1 K18

Round 33: K to the P. P1 C4F C4B P1 K18

Round 34: K to the P. P10 K 18

Round 35: K1 P1 around. P last 2 stitches together to maintain pattern.

Round 36 – 39: K1 P1 around.

Cast off *loosely*. It needs to stretch.

Make Thumb

Pick up the 13 stitches from the stitch holder. Work 3 rounds even. Cast off *loosely*.

Right Hand

Cast on 36 sts *loosely* (you need to allow the ribbing to stretch)

Round 1 – 10: K1 P1

Round 11 – 13: K around

Round 14: K1 M1 K1 M1. K19. P1 K8 P1 K5 (knitted stitches between the M1's are the thumb increase)

Round 15: K around to the P. P1 C4F C4B P1 K5

Round 16: K around to the P. P1 K8 P1 K5

Round 17: K1 M1 K3 M1 K19 P1 K8 P1 K5

Round 18: Repeat round 16

Round 19: Repeat round 16

Round 20: K1 M1 K5 M1 K19 P1 K8 P1 K5

Round 21: Repeat round 16

Round 22: Repeat round 16

Round 23: K1 M1 K7 M1 K19 P1 C4F C4B P1 K5

Round 24: K around to the P. P1 K2 P4 K2 P1 K5

Round 25: Repeat round 24

Round 26: K1 M1 K9 M1 K19 P1 K2 P4 K2 P1 K5

Round 27: Repeat round 24

Round 28: Repeat round 24

Round 29: K1 M1 K11 M1 K19 P1 K2 P4 K2 P1 K5

Round 30: Repeat round 24

Round 31: Repeat round 24

Round 32: K1 Pass the 13 stitches to the stitch holder (the thumb stitches). K19. P1 K2 P4 K2 P1 K5

Round 33: K to the P. P1 C4F C4B P1 K5

Round 34: K to the P. P10 K5

Round 35: K2tog. *P1 K1* Repeat from * to * around ending with P1.

Round 36 – 39: K1 P1 around.

Cast off *loosely*. It needs to stretch.

Make Thumb

Pick up the 13 stitches from the stitch holder. Work 3 rounds even. Cast off *loosely*.

Hints and Tips

If you need to watch the video and missed the link and QR code at the start of the pattern, here it is again. Take a pic of the square and tap the link to start watching. If you need more specific videos to help, there are specific codes for increasing and cabling in the *Abbreviations* section.

I cast all the stitches on one needle when I start. Then I divide them up between the 3 needles. This helps to avoid the twisting you can sometimes get when casting on to each needle.

Your gauge isn't overly important but best if it's at least close. Because the knitted mittens are are fingerless, they are very forgiving if they're a little small or large.

I prefer to use bamboo dpn. I find that it helps to prevent that line you get between needles when knitting in the round.

You will probably need to adjust the number of stitches you have on each needle. I usually make one split between the purl and the start of the owl motif. It gives more than 12 on one needle and less than 12 on the other, but it makes it easier to knit the owl.

I haven't tried this, but changing to even smaller needles and thinner yarn can make even smaller child sizes. Let me know if you try this and what gauge and needles give the right sizes. You can leave your findings in the comment section.

Abbreviations

K – Knit

P – Purl

K2tog – knit 2 together

sts – stitches

st – stitch

M1 – Make one (knit wise). Increase one stitch between the stitches. Pick up the yarn between the stitches. Twist it slightly and place it on your non-working needle. Knit the stitch. Watch this video on **How to M1 or Make 1** to see how.

PM1 - Make one (purl wise). Increase one stitch between the stitches. Pick up the yarn between the stitches. Twist it slightly and place it on your non-working needle. Purl the stitch. Watch this video on **How to PM1 or Purl Make 1** to see how.

Side note: I use both versions of the terminology when it comes to cable stitches. I've been corrected that I'm using the wrong one for both occasions so it's a no win for me. What I mean is that C4F is the same technique as C2F. Just like how C2B is the same as C4B. Do you think of it as the just the stitches you're pulling or the number of stitches you're using in total when you do it? It's a personal choice, I guess.

C4F - Pick up the next 2 stitches with your cable needle. Pull the stitches to the FRONT of your work. Knit the next 2 stitches on your non-working needle. Knit the 2 stitches from the cable needle. Watch this video to see how. **How to C4F or Cable 4 Forward**.

C4B - Pick up the next 2 stitches with your cable needle. Pull the stitches to the BACK of your work. Knit the next 2 stitches on your non-working needle. Knit the 2 stitches from the cable needle. Watch this video to see how. **How to C4B or Cable 4 Back**

Basic Long Fingerless Gloves

Made with large needles, these fingerless gloves are super fast to make if you know how to knit in the round. And really, knitting in the round isn't difficult. But damn, it does look impressive when you're knitting something using four needles. Not gonna lie.

But I digress. There are two styles you can make with this pattern. One has a plain cuff. The other has a double cuff. Both allow for your creativity to shine with yarn choice.

Because they are such a plain design, you can use any variety of colours to make these look awesome. Dare I say my favourite - variegated yarn - did wonders here... I really like how the splotching effect worked for the double cuff and how random the colours appeared when making the plain purl cuff with the beginning purl round.

Plain cuff with variegated yarn   *Double cuff with variegated yarn*

These also are a great stash buster. You can use up the smaller quantities of yarn from other projects to make stripes. I used the self-striping yarn available at one of the big box craft stores to make my striped version. Be warned though. Not all self-striping yarn will work for this. It needs to be smaller sections of striping than most of the self striping yarn out there. If it makes for a great ombre shawl or blanket, the striping is too wide.

If you want them longer, you can add more rows between the decrease rows. So instead of 6 rows, you could do 8 or more. If you want them to go further up the arm, cast on more when starting. Multiples of four stitches seem to work out quite nicely and let you maintain the ribbing at the fingers. I do recommend that you decrease stitches down to what's written for the various sizes. It keeps it from getting sloppy, and dare I say annoying, when they don't fit properly at the hand.

Double Cuff Fingerless Gloves

Knitting 2 together, or the decreases, do form a bit of a seam. To keep this out of view and make it run less noticeably down the inside of the arm, the pattern is designed so the thumb hole is on either side of this seam for the left and right hand.

Things You Need

Set of 4 size 9 US (5.5 mm) double pointed knitting needles (DPN)

Worsted weight yarn

Tapestry needle

Gauge

This is important to follow for correct sizing.

2" (5 cm) - 8 sts

2" (5 cm) - 11 rows

in stockinette

Left Hand (Plain Cuff)

Cast on 28 (32, 36)

Round 1 - 6: Purl around

Round 7 - 19: Knit around

Round 20: K2tog. Knit to the end of the round. You now have 27 (31, 35) sts.

Round 21 - 26: Knit around

Round 27: K2tog. Knit to the end of the round. You now have 26 (30, 34) sts.

Round 28 - 33: Knit around

Round 34: K2tog. Knit to the end of the round. You now have 25 (29, 33) sts.

Round 35 - 40: Knit around

Round 41: K2tog. Knit to the end of the round. You now have 24 (28, 32) sts.

Round 42 - 47: Knit around

Round 48: K2tog. Knit to the end of the round. You now have 23 (27, 31) sts.

Round 49 - 54: Knit around

Round 55: K2tog. Knit to the end of the round. You now have 22 (26, 30) sts.

Round 56 - 67: Knit around

Round 68: Knit 2 (4,6). Cast off 3 sts. Knit to the end of the round

Round 69: Knit 2 (4, 6). Cast on 3 sts. Knit to the end of the round. (Thumb hole made).

Round 70 - 74: P1 K1 around.

Cast off.

Right Hand (Plain Cuff)

Cast on 28 (32, 36)

Round 1 - 6: Purl around

Round 7 -19: Knit around

Round 20: K2tog. Knit to the end of the round. You now have 27 (31, 35) sts.

Round 21 - 26: Knit around

Round 27: K2tog. Knit to the end of the round. You now have 26 (30, 34) sts.

Round 28 - 33: Knit around

Round 34: K2tog. Knit to the end of the round. You now have 25 (29, 33) sts.

Round 35 - 40: Knit around

Round 41: K2tog. Knit to the end of the round. You now have 24 (28, 32) sts.

Round 42 - 47: Knit around

Round 48: K2tog. Knit to the end of the round. You now have 23 (27, 31) sts.

Round 49 - 54: Knit around

Round 55: K2tog. Knit to the end of the round. You now have 22 (26, 30) sts.

Round 56 - 67: Knit around

Round 68: Knit 17 (19, 21). Cast off 3 sts. Knit to the end of the round

Round 69: Knit 17 (19, 21). Cast on 3 sts. Knit to the end of the round. (Thumb hole made).

Round 70 - 74: K1 P1 around.

Cast off.

Left Hand (Double Cuff)

Cast on 28 (32, 36)

Round 1 - 6: Purl around

Round 7 - 15: Knit around (If you are going to change the colour of the yarn for the purl rows, knit round 15 with the new colour).

Round 16 - 19: Purl around

Round 20: K2tog. Knit to the end of the round. You now have 27 (31, 35) sts.

Round 21 - 26: Knit around

Round 27: K2tog. Knit to the end of the round. You now have 26 (30, 34) sts.

Round 28 - 33: Knit around

Round 34: K2tog. Knit to the end of the round. You now have 25 (29, 33) sts.

Round 35 - 40: Knit around

Round 41: K2tog. Knit to the end of the round. You now have 24 (28, 32) sts.

Round 42 - 47: Knit around

Round 48: K2tog. Knit to the end of the round. You now have 23 (27, 31) sts.

Round 49 - 54: Knit around

Round 55: K2tog. Knit to the end of the round. You now have 22 (26, 30) sts.

Round 56 - 67: Knit around

Round 68: Knit 2 (4,6). Cast off 3 sts. Knit to the end of the round

Round 69: Knit 2 (4, 6). Cast on 3 sts. Knit to the end of the round. (Thumb hole made).

Round 70 - 74: P1 K1 around.

Cast off.

Right Hand (Double Cuff)

Cast on 28 (32, 36)

Round 1 - 6: Purl around

Round 7 - 15: Knit around (If you are going to change the colour of the yarn for the purl rows, knit round 15 with the new colour).

Round 16 - 19: Purl around

Round 20: K2tog. Knit to the end of the round. You now have 27 (31, 35) sts.

Round 21 - 26: Knit around

Round 27: K2tog. Knit to the end of the round. You now have 26 (30, 34) sts.

Round 28 - 33: Knit around

Round 34: K2tog. Knit to the end of the round. You now have 25 (29, 33) sts.

Round 35 - 40: Knit around

Round 41: K2tog. Knit to the end of the round. You now have 24 (28, 32) sts.

Round 42 - 47: Knit around

Round 48: K2tog. Knit to the end of the round. You now have 23 (27, 31) sts.

Round 49 - 54: Knit around

Round 55: K2tog. Knit to the end of the round. You now have 22 (26, 30) sts.

Round 56 - 67: Knit around

Round 68: Knit 17 (19, 21). Cast off 3 sts. Knit to the end of the round

Round 69: Knit 17 (19, 21). Cast on 3 sts. Knit to the end of the round. (Thumb hole made).

Round 70 - 74: K1 P1 around.

Cast off.

Plain cuff gloves with stripe pattern

Abbreviations

K – knit

P – purl

K2tog – Knit 2 together

st – sttch

sts - stitches

Cable Fingerless Gloves or Mitts

The season is getting colder again, the few apples on my trees are turning red and my mind turns back towards knitting. And oh boy, am I coming up with a bunch of knitting designs! Now here's to finding the time to publish them all. Work is also back to full-time so that's great news.

A couple of things about this knitting pattern before we grab our favourite worsted weight yarn, double pointed and cable needles and get to work. Like my **Owl Fingerless Gloves** pattern, I am keeping the stitch count the same and only changing the needles size to change the size of the glove. The pattern on the back of the hand stays proportional in size and placement on the glove remains the same for a better overall look.

I made a number of different lengths of the glove too, for demonstrative purposes. The taupe with flecks (apparently it's also known as tweed, who knew) is the pattern exactly as written. I repeated the cable pattern once for the grey pair and 4 times for the purple tweed/flecked. There's a note in the pattern what rows make up the 5 plait cable pattern. Why do 3 cables when you can do 5? I've always been a bit of an overachiever

Ok. Enough of that. Let's get knitting!!!

Things You Need

Worsted weight yarn – (any standard ball will be more than enough to make the shorter, hand only version. You'll need more if you are making them longer. For example, I used less than a 100 gr or 3.5 oz ball to make the long purple gloves in size small.)

Set of 4 double pointed needles (see *Gauge* section)

Stitch holder

Tapestry needle to sew the hole by the thumb and work in ends

Cable needle

Gauge

Small

size 4 mm (US size 6) dpn
10 stitches every 2 inches (5 cm)
13 rows every 2 inches (5 cm)

Medium

size 5 mm (US size 8) dpn
9 stitches every 2 inches (5 cm)
12 rows every 2 inches (5 cm)

Large

size 6 mm (US size 10) dpn
8 stitches every 2 inches (5 cm)
11 rows every 2 inches (5 cm)

Left Hand

Cast on 36

Row 1-8: K1 P1 around

Row 9: K4 P1 K15 P1 K15

Row 10: K4 P1 C6F twice. K3 P1 K15 (go to the abbreviations section for a description of how to make C6F)

Row 11 – 12: as row 9

Row 13: K4 P1 K3 C6B twice. P1 K15 (go to the abbreviations section for a description of how to make C6B)

Row 14 – 15: as row 9

Rows 10 to 15 make the cable pattern. Repeat these rows to make the gloves longer as described earlier.

Next Row: K1 M1 K1 M1 K2 P1 C6F twice K3 P1 K15 (38 sts)

Next *2* Rows: K6 P1 K15 P1 K15

Next Row: K1 M1 K3 M1 K2 P1 K3 C6B twice P1 K15 (40 sts)

Next *2* Rows: K8 P1 K15 P1 K15

Next Row: K1 M1 K5 M1 K2 P1 C6F twice K3 P1 K15 (42 sts)

Next *2* Rows: K10 P1 K15 P1 K15

Next Row: K1 M1 K7 M1 K2 P1 K3 C6B twice P1 K15 (44 sts)

Next *2* Rows: K12 P1 K15 P1 K15

Next Row: K1 M1 K9 M1 K2 P1 C6F twice K3 P1 K15 (46 sts)

Next *2* Rows: K14 P1 K15 P1 K15

Next Row: K1 M1 K11 M1 K2 P1 K3 C6B twice P1 K15 (48 sts)

Next *2* Rows: K16 P1 K15 P1 K15

Next Row: K1 Pass the next 13 stitches onto a stitch holder. K2 P1 C6F twice K3 P1 K15 (35 sts)

Next Row: K3 P1 K15 P1 K15

Next Row: K1 P1 around to last 2 sts. P2tog

Next *4* Rows: K1 P1 around

Cast off *loosely*.

Make Thumb

Pick up the 13 stitches from the stitch holder. Work 3 rounds even. Cast off *loosely*.

Right Hand

Cast on 36

Row 1-8: K1 P1 around

Row 9: K18 P1 K15 P1 K1

Row 10: K18 P1 C6F twice K3 P1 K1

Row 11 – 12: as row 9

Row 13: K18 P1 K3 C6B twice P1 K1

Row 14 – 15: as row 9

Rows 10 to 15 make the cable pattern. Repeat these rows to make the gloves longer as described earlier.

Next Row: K1 M1 K1 M1 K16 P1 C6F twice K3 P1 K1 (38 sts)

Next 2 Rows: K20 P1 K15 P1 K1

Next Row: K1 M1 K3 M1 K16 P1 K3 C6B twice P1 K1 (40 sts)

Next 2 Rows: K22 P1 K15 P1 K1

Next Row: K1 M1 K5 M1 K16 P1 C6F twice K3 P1 K1 (42 sts)

Next 2 Rows: K24 P1 K15 P1 K1

Next Row: K1 M1 K7 M1 K16 P1 K3 C6B twice P1 K1 (44 sts)

Next 2 Rows: K26 P1 K15 P1 K1

Next Row: K1 M1 K9 M1 K16 P1 C6F twice K3 P1 K1 (46 sts)

Next 2 Rows: K28 P1 K15 P1 K1

Next Row: K1 M1 K11 M1 K16 P1 K3 C6B twice P1 K1 (48 sts)

Next 2 Rows: K30 P1 K15 P1 K1

Next Row: K1 Pass the next 13 stitches onto a stitch holder. K16 P1 C6F twice K3 P1 K1 (35 sts)

Next Row: K17 P1 K15 P1 K1

Next Row: K1 P1 around to last 2 sts. P2tog

Next 4 Rows: K1 P1 around

Cast off *loosely.*

Make Thumb

Pick up the 13 stitches from the stitch holder. Work 3 rounds even. Cast off *loosely.*

Hints and Tips

C6F and C6B are VERY similar to C4F and C4B. The only difference is the number of stitches you pull forward and pull back, respectively. If you started with this pattern, look back to the owl gloves to see the QR code that shows you how to do the C4F and C4B. I never made a video specifically for these 2 techniques. Sorry.

If you have too many stitches double check to make sure you haven't picked up a stitch between the needles. If you don't have enough stitches, did you drop one when you were making the cable?

I cast all the stitches on one needle when I start. Then I divide them up between the 3 needles. This helps to avoid the twisting you can sometimes get when casting on to each needle.

I prefer to use bamboo dpn. I find that it helps to prevent that line you get between needles when knitting in the round.

You will probably need to adjust the number of stitches you have on each needle. I usually make one split between the purl and the start of the cable motif with one needle having 15 stitches. It gives more than 12 on one needle and less than 12 on the other, but it makes it easier to knit the cable.

If you like your ribbing to be a little more snug, you can use a smaller size needles to knit this portion. Stepping it down a half size; small – 3.5 mm, medium – 4.5 mm and large 5.5 mm should work. You may want to go smaller. I don't do this because I always forget to switch back.

I haven't tried this, but changing to even smaller needles and thinner yarn can make even smaller child sizes. Let me know if you try this and what gauge and needles give the right sizes.

Abbreviations

K – Knit

P – Purl

Sts – stitches

P2tog – Purl 2 together

C6F – Cable 6 forward. With your cable needle, slip 3 stitches off the needle and pull the stitches towards the *front* of your work. Knit the next 3 stitches. Knit the 3 stitches from the cable needle.

C6B – Cable 6 backward. With your cable needle, slip 3 stitches off the needle and pull the stitches to the *back* of your work. Knit the next 3 stitches. Knit the 3 stitches from the cable needle.

M1 – Make one (knit wise). Increase one stitch between the stitches. Pick up the yarn between the stitches. Twist slightly. Place it on your non-working needle. Knit the stitch. Click this link to watch this video to see how. **How to Make One or M1 – Increase between stitches** or take a pic of the QR code below with your phone or tablet. Tap the link that pops up.

Knit a Pair of Flip Mittens or Fingerless Gloves

Make yourself a nifty pair of flip mitts. They're hip, trendy and handier than a pocket on a shirt! Not only can you make these super awesome mitts for just about anyone from teen to adult, but you can forgo the finger portion and make some cool fingerless gloves.Technically, they're fingerless mittens but that just sounds weird.

They're knitted on double point needles, also known as DPN. Though this sounds intimidating, it really is very simple. You'll need to know how to knit to make this project, but knitting in the round is the same as knitting flat. Only difference is you don't flip your work back in forth; it's done a continuous circle.

The sizing for mittens, like socks or slippers, is somewhat general. The small size will fit someone with a smaller hand, medium is an average lady's hand, large is for an average man's hand, and extra large will fit a very large man's hand.

Things You Need

Yarn (a standard ball of worsted weight yarn will be more than enough)

Size 5 mm (US size 8) double pointed needles (or whatever size needles you need to get the correct gauge).

Stitch holder

Hook and loop fastener (AKA - Velcro*)

Glue

Gauge

In stockinette

18 stitches = 4 inches
24 rows = 4 inches

Small

The Mitt

Cast on 28 sts (loosely). Divide these evenly as possible on three of the double pointed needles.

Round 1 - 12: K2, P2 (Creates knit 2 purl 2 ribbing).

Round 13 - 17: Knit

Round 18: K1, M1, k1, M1. K26.

Round 19 - 20: Knit

Round 21: K1, M1, k3, M1. K26.

Round 22 - 23: Knit

Round 24: K1, M1, k5, M1. K26.

Round 25 - 26: Knit

Round 27: K1, M1, k7, M1. K26.

Round 28 - 29: Knit

Round 30: K1, M1, k9, M1. K26.

Round 31 - 32: Knit

Round 33: K1, place next 11 sts onto the stitch holder. K26.

Round 34: K1, M1, K26.

Round 35 - 37: Knit

Round 38 – 42: K2, P2

Bind off loosely.

The Thumb

Worked over the 11 sts on the stitch holder.

Pick up and divided the 11 sts on the stitch holder between the 3 double pointed needles. One of the needles will have more sts than the others.

Round 1 – 12: Knit

Round 13: K2tog around. (You may have to pass the last stitch from one dpn the next dpn to do this).

Round 14: Knit

Pull yarn through.

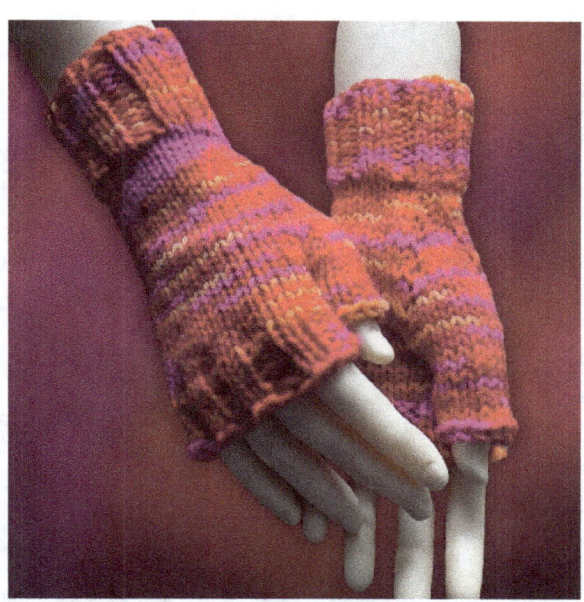

Medium

The Mitt

Cast on 32 sts (loosely). Divide these evenly as possible on three of the double pointed needles

Round 1 - 12: K2, P2 (Creates knit 2 purl 2 ribbing).

Round 13 - 17: Knit

Round 18: K1, M1, k1, M1. K30.

Round 19 - 20: Knit

Round 21: K1, M1, k3, M1. K30.

Round 22 - 23: Knit

Round 24: K1, M1, k5, M1. K30.

Round 25 - 26: Knit

Round 27: K1, M1, k7, M1. K30.

Round 28 - 29: Knit

Round 30: K1, M1, k9, M1. K30.

Round 31 - 32: Knit

Round 33: K1, M1, k11, M1. K30.

Round 34 - 35: Knit

Round 36: K1, place next 13 sts onto the stitch holder. K30.

Round 37: K1, M1, K30.

Round 38 - 40: Knit

Round 41 – 45: K2, P2

Bind off loosely.

The Thumb

Worked over the 13 sts on the stitch holder.

Pick up and divided the 13 sts on the stitch holder between the 3 double pointed needles. One of the needles will have more sts than the others.

Round 1 – 13: Knit

Round 14: K2tog around. (You may have to pass the last stitch from one dpn the next dpn to do this).

Round 15: Knit

Pull yarn through.

Large

The Mitt

Cast on 36 sts (loosely). Divide these evenly as possible on three of the double pointed needles.

Round 1 - 12: K2, P2 (Creates knit 2 purl 2 ribbing).

Round 13 - 17: Knit

Round 18: K1, M1, k1, M1. K34.

Round 19 - 20: Knit

Round 21: K1, M1, k3, M1. K34.

Round 22 - 23: Knit

Round 24: K1, M1, k5, M1. K34.

Round 25 - 26: Knit

Round 27: K1, M1, k7, M1. K34.

Round 28 - 29: Knit

Round 30: K1, M1, k9, M1. K34.

Round 31 - 32: Knit

Round 33: K1, M1, k11, M1. K34.

Round 34 - 35: Knit

Round 36: K1, M1, k13, M1. K34.

Round 37 - 38: Knit

Round 39: K1, place next 15 sts onto the stitch holder. K34.

Round 40: K1, M1, K34.

Round 41 - 43: Knit

Round 44 - 49: K2, P2

Bind off loosely.

The Thumb

Worked over the 15 sts on the stitch holder.

Pick up and divided the 15 sts on the stitch holder between the 3 double pointed needles. One of the needles will have more sts than the others.

Round 1 – 18: Knit

Round 19: K2tog around. (You may have to pass the last stitch from one dpn the next dpn to do this).

Round 20: Knit

Pull yarn through.

Extra Large

The Mitt

Cast on 40 sts (loosely). Divide these evenly as possible on three of the double pointed needles.

Round 1 - 12: K2, P2 (Creates knit 2 purl 2 ribbing).

Round 13 - 17: Knit

Round 18: K1, M1, k1, M1. K38.

Round 19 - 20: Knit

Round 21: K1, M1, k3, M1. K38.

Round 22 - 23: Knit

Round 24: K1, M1, k5, M1. K38.

Round 25 - 26: Knit

Round 27: K1, M1, k7, M1. K38.

Round 28 - 29: Knit

Round 30: K1, M1, k9, M1. K38.

Round 31 - 32: Knit

Round 33: K1, M1, k11, M1. K38.

Round 34 - 35: Knit

Round 36: K1, M1, k13, M1. K38.

Round 37-38: Knit

Round 39: K1, M1, k15, M1. K38.

Round 40 – 41: Knit

Round 42: K1, place next 17 sts onto the stitch holder. K38.

Round 43: K1, M1, K38.

Round 44 - 46: Knit

Round 47 - 52: K2, P2

Bind off loosely.

The Thumb

Worked over the 17 sts on the stitch holder.

Pick up and divided the 17 sts on the stitch holder between the 3 double pointed needles. One of the needles will have more sts than the others.

Round 1 – 20: Knit

Round 21: K2tog around. (You may have to pass the last stitch from one dpn the next dpn to do this).

Round 22: Knit

Pull yarn through.

Finger Flap

Instructions are written for small (**medium,** large, extra **large**)

Cast on 32 (**36,** 40, **44**) loosely.

Round 1 – 6: K2 P2

Round 7 and on: Knit around until work measures 3 (3.5, 4, 4.5) inches from the cast on edge.

Next round: K1 K2tog K10 (**12,** 14, **16**) K2 tog K2 K2tog K10 (**12,** 14, **16**) K2tog K1.

Next 2 rounds: Knit

Next round: K1 K2tog K8 (**10,** 12, **14**) K2 tog K2 K2tog K8 (**10,** 12, **14**) K2tog K1.

Next 2 rounds: Knit

Next round: K1 K2tog K6 (**8,** 10, **12**) K2 tog K2 K2tog K6 (**8,** 10, **12**) K2tog K1.

Next 2 rounds: Knit

Next round: K1 K2tog K4 (**6,** 8, **10**) K2 tog K2 K2tog K4 (**6,** 8, **10**) K2tog K1.

Next 2 rounds: Knit

Transfer the stitches onto two needles being sure that the thumb is along the edge of fold.

Break yarn leaving enough to graft the fingertips and sew in ends. 12 inches is plenty.

How to Graft the Fingertips

The divided stitches will look something like this:

With a darning needle, insert the needle through the front loop of the first needle as if to **PURL**.

Insert needle through the stitch on the back needle as shown.

Insert the needle through the back loop of the first stitch AND through the stitch of the next stitch as if to **PURL**. Drop the first stitch.

Insert the needle through the stitch on the back needle as if to **PURL**. Drop this stitch.

*Insert the needle through the back loop of the next stitch on the front needle and the front loop of the next stitch as if to **PURL**. Drop the first stitch.

Insert the needle through the stitch on the back needle as if to **PURL**. Drop this stitch.

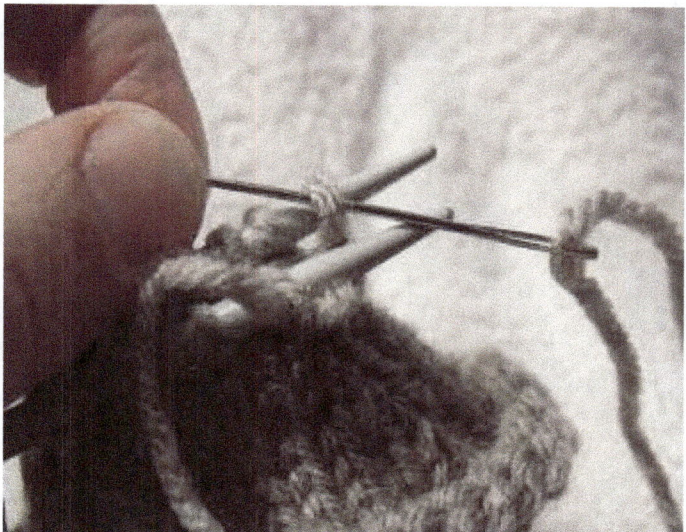

Repeat from * until there are no stitches left on either needle.

Pull the yarn tight.

Make another mitten to match.

Attaching the Velcro

Cut a small piece of Velcro. Keeping both halves of the Velcro together, attach it to the back of the mitten first. Glue it in place.

Keeping the Velcro pieces together, place some glue on the other half of the Velcro. Pull the finger flap back (off the fingers). Press firmly. DO NOT pull the Velcro apart until ALL the glue has dried completely.

Abbreviations

K – Knit

P – Purl

K2tog – knit 2 together

sts – stitches

st – stitch

M1 – Make one (knit wise). Increase one stitch between the stitches. Pick up the yarn between the stitches. Twist it slightly and place it on your non-working needle. Knit the stitch. Watch this video on **How to M1 or Make 1** to see how.

Hints and Tips

You don't need a stitch holder. Even a piece of yarn will work.

Instead of glue, you can also sew the Velcro on. I find glue is simpler and quicker.

Customize this pattern as you see fit. If you want the cuff longer, do so. If you need a longer thumb or finger flap, add more rows. As long as your stitch counts stay the same, it should work out fine.

Some folks like to felt their mittens as it can help stop the wind from blowing through the stitches. Be careful though because felting shrinks your work! It's hard to guess how much shrinkage will happen as there are so many variables involved, from temperature of the water to how much agitation occurs during the felting process. You can give it a try but make sure you use PURE wool! Anything that is a blend won't felt properly. My last attempt at felting a pair of mittens for myself resulted in my young son getting a new pair of mitts. At least they didn't go to waste :-/

Knit a Pair
of Texting Mitts

Improve your texting in cold climates with these thumbless mittens. More than just a pair of fingerless gloves, these keep your hands warm and only expose your thumbs when needed. The thumb pocket is sewn on and the flap is secured at the base of the palm with Velcro* for easy access. The flap hangs in the back out of the way to enable your texting abilities. Plan on using your thumbs for a while? Then simply tuck the flap into the thumb pocket.

The sizes are each written separately as each size is a bit different in row and stitch counts. Medium fits the average lady's hand, large for men, and small for pre-teens.

Things You Need

Yarn (a standard ball of worsted weight yarn will be more than enough)

Size 4.5 mm double pointed needles

Stitch holder

Hook and loop fastener (AKA - Velcro)

Glue

Gauge

In stockinette
10 stitches = 2 inches
13 rows = 2 inches

Small

The Mitt

Cast on 32 sts (loosely). Divide these evenly as possible on three of the double pointed needles.

Round 1 – 15: K2, P2 (Creates knit 2 purl 2 ribbing).

Round 16 - 18: Knit

Round 19: K1, M1, k1, M1 Knit remaining sts.

Round 20 – 21: Knit

Round 22: K1, M1, k3, M1. Knit remaining sts.

Round 23 – 24: Knit

Round 25: K1, M1, k5, M1. Knit remaining sts.

Round 26 – 27: Knit

Round 28: K1, M1, k7, M1. Knit remaining sts.

Round 29 – 30: Knit

Round 31: K1, M1, k9, M1. Knit remaining sts.

Round 32 – 33: Knit

Round 34: K1, place next 11 sts onto the stitch holder. Knit the remaining sts.. There should be 31 sts divided on the three needles.

Round 35 and on: Knit in the round on these remaining 31 sts until work measures approximately 3.5 inches from the stitches held back to form the thumb.

Form Fingertips

Next round: K1, k2tog, K10 K2tog, K2, K2tog, K9, K2tog, K1.

Next two rounds: Knit

Next round: K1, K2tog, K8, K2 tog, K2, K2tog, K7, K2tog, K1.

Next two rounds: Knit

Next round: K1, K2tog, K6, K2 tog, K2, K2tog, K5, K2tog, K1.

Next two rounds: Knit

Transfer the stitches onto two needles being sure that the stitches held back for the thumb are along the fold.

Break yarn leaving enough to graft the fingertips and sew in ends. 12 inches is plenty.

Finishing the Thumb

Worked over the 11 sts on the stitch holder. Leave the end you attach to complete the thumb longer than you normally would. You can use this to sew the thumb flap onto the mitten.

Pick up and divided the 11 sts on the stitch holder between the 3 double pointed needles. One of the needles will have more sts than the others.

Round 1 – 5: Knit

Bind off loosely.

Thumb Flap

Using 2 of your double pointed needles and working back and forth.

Cast on 3 sts.

Row 1: Knit

Row 2: Purl

Row 3: K1, M1, K1 M1, K1. (5 sts)

Row 4: Purl

Row 5: Knit

Row 6: Purl

Row 7: Knit

Row 8: Purl

Row 9: K1, M1, K3, M1, K1. (7 sts)

Row 10: Purl

Row 11: Knit

Row 12: Purl

Row 13: Knit

Row 14: Purl

Row 15: With the right side of your work facing you, cast on 3 sts. Working over the 3 sts you just cast on, K3. Leave these 3 sts on the needle you used to knit them. With another double pointed needle, knit the 7 sts from the previous row. With the wrong side of you work facing you, cast on 3 sts. Transfer these 3 sts onto another double pointed needle. You will now start knitting in the round.

With the right side of your work facing you:

Round 16 – 25: Knit

Round 28: K2tog, K1, K2 tog 3 times, K1, K2tog, K1 .

Round 29: Knit

Round 30: K2tog four times

Draw loops together and sew in the ends.

Medium

The Mitt

Cast on 36 sts (loosely). Divide these evenly on three of the double pointed needles.

Round 1 – 15: K2, P2 (Creates knit 2 purl 2 ribbing).

Round 16 - 18: Knit

Round 19: K1, M1, k1, M1. Knit remaining sts.

Round 20 – 21: Knit

Round 22: K1, M1, k3, M1. Knit remaining sts.

Round 23 – 24: Knit

Round 25: K1, M1, k5, M1. Knit remaining sts.

Round 26 – 27: Knit

Round 28: K1, M1, k7, M1. Knit remaining sts.

Round 29 – 30: Knit

Round 31: K1, M1, k9, M1. Knit remaining sts.

Round 32 – 33: Knit

Round 34: K1, M1, k11, M1. Knit remaining sts.

Round 35 – 36: Knit

Round 37: K1, place next 13 sts onto the stitch holder. Knit the remaining sts. There should be 35 sts divided on the three needles.

Round 38 and on: Knit in the round on these remaining 35 sts until work measures approximately 4 inches from the stitches held back to form the thumb.

Form Fingertips

Next round: K1, k2tog, K12 K2tog, K2, K2tog, K11, K2tog, K1.

Next two rounds: Knit

Next round: K1, K2tog, K10, K2 tog, K2, K2tog, K9, K2tog, K1.

Next two rounds: Knit

Next round: K1, K2tog, K8, K2 tog, K2, K2tog, K7, K2tog, K1.

Next two rounds: Knit

Transfer the stitches onto two needles being sure that the stitches held back for the thumb are along the fold.

Break yarn leaving enough to graft the fingertips and sew in ends. 12 inches is plenty.

Finishing the Thumb

Worked over the 13 sts on the stitch holder. Leave the end you attach to complete the thumb longer than you normally would. You can use this to sew the thumb flap onto the mitten.

Pick up and divided the 13 sts on the stitch holder between the 3 double pointed needles. One of the needles will have more sts than the others.

Round 1 – 5: Knit

Bind off loosely.

Thumb Flap

Using 2 of your double pointed needles and working back and forth.

Cast on 3 sts.

Row 1: Knit

Row 2: Purl

Row 3: K1, M1, K1 M1, K1. (5 sts)

Row 4: Purl

Row 5: Knit

Row 6: Purl

Row 7: Knit

Row 8: Purl

Row 9: K1, M1, K3, M1, K1. (7 sts)

Row 10: Purl

Row 11: Knit

Row 12: Purl

Row 13: Knit

Row 14: Purl

Row 15: With the right side of your work facing you, cast on 5 sts. Working over the 5 sts you just cast on, K5. Leave these 5 sts on the needle you used to knit them. With another double pointed needle, knit the 7 sts from the previous row. With the wrong side of you work facing you, cast on 5 sts. Transfer these 5 sts onto another double pointed needle. You will now start knitting in the round.

With the right side of your work facing you:

Round 16 – 27: Knit

Round 28: K2tog twice, K1, K2 tog 3 times, K1, K2 tog twice, K1.

Round 29: Knit

Round 30: K2tog, K1, K2tog twice, K2tog, K1

Draw loops together and sew in the ends.

Large

The Mitt

Cast on 40 sts (loosely). Divide these evenly as possible on three of the double pointed needles.

Round 1 – 15: K2, P2 (Creates knit 2 purl 2 ribbing).

Round 16 - 18: Knit

Round 19: K1, M1, k1, M1. Knit remaining sts.

Round 20 – 21: Knit

Round 22: K1, M1, k3, M1. Knit remaining sts.

Round 23 – 24: Knit

Round 25: K1, M1, k5, M1. Knit remaining sts.

Round 26 – 27: Knit

Round 28: K1, M1, k7, M1. Knit remaining sts.

Round 29 – 30: Knit

Round 31: K1, M1, k9, M1. Knit remaining sts.

Round 32 – 33: Knit

Round 34: K1, M1, k11, M1. Knit remaining sts.

Round 35 – 36: Knit

Round 37: K1, M1, k13, M1. Knit remaining sts.

Round 38 – 39: Knit

Round 40: K1, place next 15 sts onto the stitch holder. Knit the remaining sts. There should be 39 sts divided on the three needles.

Round 41 and on: Knit in the round on these remaining 39 sts until work measures approximately 5 inches from the stitches held back to form the thumb.

Form Fingertips

Next round: K1, k2tog, K14 K2tog, K2, K2tog, K13, K2tog, K1.

Next two rounds: Knit

Next round: K1, K2tog, K12, K2 tog, K2, K2tog, K11, K2tog, K1.

Next two rounds: Knit

Next round: K1, K2tog, K10, K2 tog, K2, K2tog, K9, K2tog, K1.

Next two rounds: Knit

Transfer the stitches onto two needles being sure that the stitches held back for the thumb are along the fold.

Break yarn leaving enough to graft the fingertips and sew in ends. 12 inches is plenty.

Finishing the Thumb

Worked over the 15 sts on the stitch holder. Leave the end you attach to complete the thumb longer than you normally would. You can use this to sew the thumb flap onto the mitten.

Pick up and divided the 15 sts on the stitch holder between the 3 double pointed needles. One of the needles will have more sts than the others.

Round 1 – 8: Knit

Bind off loosely.

Thumb Flap

Using 2 of your double pointed needles and working back and forth.

Cast on 3 sts.

Row 1: Knit

Row 2: Purl

Row 3: K1, M1, K1 M1, K1. (5 sts)

Row 4: Purl

Row 5: Knit

Row 6: Purl

Row 7: Knit

Row 8: Purl

Row 9: K1, M1, K3, M1, K1. (7 sts)

Row 10: Purl

Row 11: Knit

Row 12: Purl

Row 13: Knit

Row 14: Purl

Row 15: K1, M1, K5, M1, K1. (9 sts)

Row 16: Purl

Row 17: Knit

Row 18: Purl

Row 19: Knit

Row 20: Purl

Row 21: With the right side of your work facing you, cast on 5 sts. Working over the 5 sts you just cast on, K5. Leave these 5 sts on the needle you used to knit them. With another double pointed needle, knit the 9 sts from the previous row. With the wrong side of you work facing you, cast on 5 sts. Transfer these 5 sts onto another double pointed needle. You will now start knitting in the round. With the right side of your work facing you:

Round 22 – 38: Knit

Round 39: K2tog twice, K1, K2 tog 4 times, K1, K2 tog twice, K1.

Round 40: Knit

Round 41: K2tog, K1, K2tog twice, K1, K2tog, K1

Draw loops together and sew in the ends.

How to Graft the Fingertips

The divided sts will look something like this:

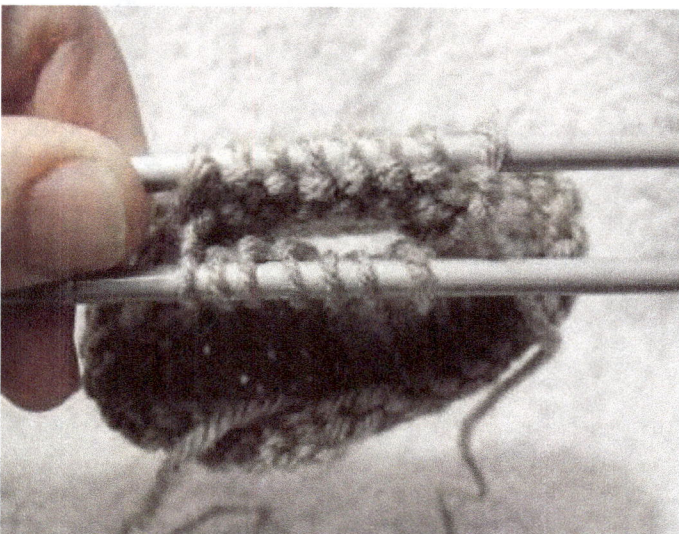

With a darning needle, insert the needle through the front loop of the first needle as if to **PURL**.

Insert needle through the stitch on the back needle as shown.

Insert the needle through the back loop of the first stitch AND through the stitch of the next stitch as if to **PURL**. Drop the first stitch.

Insert the needle through the stitch on the back needle as if to **PURL**. Drop this stitch.

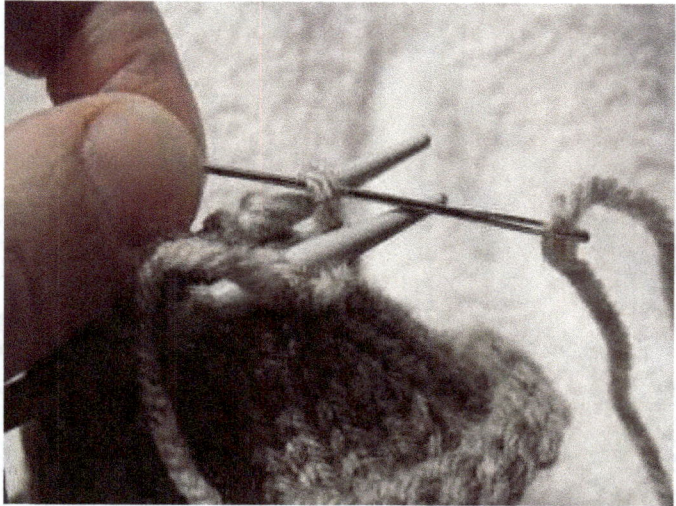

*Insert the needle through the back loop of the next stitch on the front needle and the front loop of the next stitch as if to **PURL**. Drop the first stitch.

Insert the needle through the stitch on the back needle as if to **PURL**. Drop this stitch.

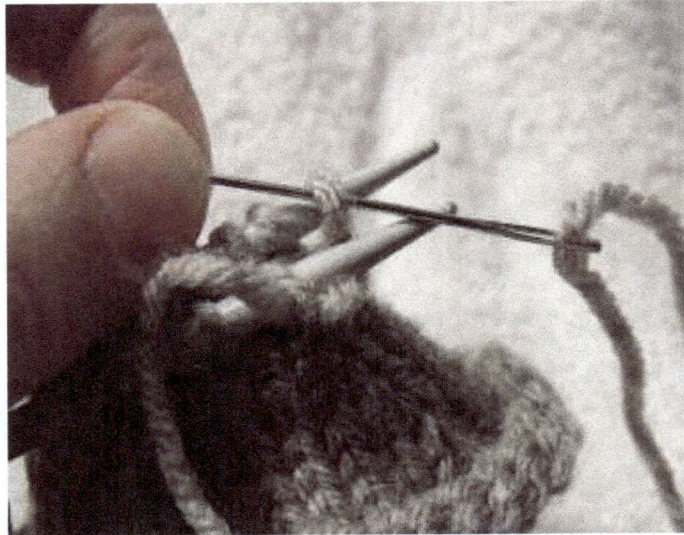

Repeat from * until there are no stitches left on either needle.

Pull the yarn tight.

Make another mitten to match.

Attaching the Thumb Flap

With the yarn left from where you continued the thumb, attach the thumb flap to the mitten. Make sure that you attach the thumb flap to the back side of the left and right mittens accordingly. Easiest way is to lay the mitts flat with the thumbs pointing in opposite directions.

Attaching the Velcro

Cut a small piece of Velcro that will fit on the base of the thumb flap. Keeping both halves of the Velcro together, attach it to the THUMB FLAP first. Glue it in place.

Keeping the Velcro pieces together, place some glue on the other half of the Velcro. Pull the thumb flap forward in the toasty warm thumb position. With the Velcro still together, place the Velcro where the bottom of the flap touches the palm of the mitten. Press firmly. DO NOT pull the Velcro apart until ALL the glue has dried completely.

Abbreviations

K – Knit

P – Purl

K2tog – knit 2 together

sts – stitches

st – stitch

M1 – Make one (knit wise). Increase one stitch between the stitches. Pick up the yarn between the stitches. Twist it slightly and place it on your non-working needle. Knit the stitch. Watch this video on **How to M1 or Make 1** to see how.

Hints and Tips

Make sure when attaching the Velcro to the thumb flap, that the fuzzy half of the Velcro is what you use for the flap. In other words, which ever side feels less rough. The other pokey side should go on the palm of the mitt. That way the Velcro won't stick to the inside of the thumb flap when folded back into itself.

When picking up stitches to finish the thumb on the mitt, leave a long piece of yarn to sew on the thumb flap. This saves on the number of ends to sew in when you're done.

You don't need a stitch holder. Even a piece of yarn will work.

Instead of glue, you can also sew the Velcro on. I find glue is simpler and quicker.

How to Knit Arm Warmers or Gloves – with BOWS!

Knit a fabulous pair of fingerless gloves or arm warmers with the cutest little bows flowing down the length of your arm and back of your hand. Create the bows as you go; I have pics to show you how. Make them into arm warmers or as short gloves. It really depends on how much you like knitting in the round on double pointed needles (DPN).

Like the owl motif, I have a love affair going on with these bows. So far, I've incorporated it into slippers and a dishcloth, both of which are available to read on my website for free at **KweenBee.com**

A few quick words on sizing. Instead of going through all the effort to remake the pattern for different sizes and having the bows remain centred, I've gone about adjusting the sizing by changing the size of your knitting needles. These mitts knitted in the round making them seamless with no scratchy seams to worry about. Because of being knitted in the round, the thumbs have to be on different sides so they fit correctly. You'll have to make one for the left hand and the right hand. Instructions are given separately for both.

Things You Need

Worsted weight yarn (any standard ball will be more than enough to make the shorter, hand only version. You'll need more if you are making them longer. For example, I used less than a 100 gr or 3.5 oz ball to make the long green gloves in size medium.)

Set of 4 double pointed needles (see *Gauge* section)

Stitch holder

Tapestry needle to sew the hole by the thumb and work in end.

Gauge

In *stockinette* stitch

Small

size 3.5 mm (US size 4) single pointed needles
11 stitches every 2 inches (5 cm)
16 rows every 2 inches (5 cm)

Medium

size 4 mm (US size 6) single pointed needles
10 stitches every 2 inches (5 cm)
14 rows every 2 inches (5 cm)

Large

size 5 mm (US size 8) single pointed needles
9 stitches every 2 inches (5 cm)
12 rows every 2 inches (5 cm)

Left Hand

Cast on 36 sts *loosely*. You need to allow the ribbing to stretch.

Rounds 1 - 7: K1 P1 around

Rounds 8 - 9: K around

🐾 **Round 10:** K8 P1 Hold the yarn in front of your work. Pass the next 7 stitches over to the other needle (strand made). P1 K19. Be sure to leave some slack in the strand as shown.

Round 11: K8 P1 K7 P1 K19

Round 12: As round 10

Round 13: As round 11

Round 14: As round 10

Round 15: As round 11

Round 16: As round 10

Round 17: As round 11

Round 18: K8 P1 K3 Pick up the 4 strands from the bottom up

And knit the next stitch.

Pull the loop down through the 4 strands

Bow completed (2nd photo shows additional K3 completed)

K3 P1 K19

Round 18 written without photos: K8 P1 K3 Pick up the 4 strands from the bottom up and knit the next stitch. Pull the loop down through the 4 strands (Bow completed). K3 P1 K19

Round 19: K8 P1 K7 P1 K19 🐱

Repeat from 🐱 to 🐱 if you would like a longer length of glove. Each 🐱 to 🐱 repeat makes 1 bow motif.

Round 20: K1 M1 K1 M1 K6 P1 Hold the yarn in front of your work. Pass the next 7 stitches over to the other needle (strand made). P1 K19

Round 21: K to the P. P1 K7 P1 K19

Round 22: K to the P. P1 Hold the yarn in front of your work. Pass the next 7 stitches over to the other needle (strand made). P1 K19

Round 23: K1 M1 K3 M1 K6 P1 K7 P1 K19

Round 24: As round 22

Round 25: As round 21

Round 26: K1 M1 K5 M1 K6 P1 Hold the yarn in front of your work. Pass the next 7 stitches over to the other needle (strand made). P1 K19

Round 27: As round 21

Round 28: K to the P. P1 K3 Pick up the 4 strands from the bottom up and knit the next stitch. Pull the loop down through the 4 strands (Bow completed). K3 P1 K19

Round 29: K1 M1 K7 M1 K6 P1 K7 P1 K19

Round 30: As round 22

Round 31: As round 21

Round 32: K1 M1 K9 M1 K6 P1 Hold the yarn in front of your work. Pass the next 7 stitches over to the other needle (strand made). P1 K19

Round 33: As round 21

Round 34: As round 22

Round 35: K1 M1 K11 M1 K6 P1 K7 P1 K19

Round 36: As round 22

Round 37: As round 21

Round 38: K1 Pass next 13 stitches onto the stitch holder. K6 P1 K3. Pick up the 4 strands from the bottom up and knit the next stitch. Pull the loop down through the 4 strands (Bow completed). K3 P1 K19

Round 39: As round 21

Rounds 40 – 41: K around

Round 42: K2tog P1 K1 around. P1 in last stitch.

Round 43 – 46: K1 P1 around.

Cast off *loosely*.

Make Thumb

Pick up the 13 stitches from the stitch holder. Work 3 rounds even.

Cast off *loosely*.

Sew in the ends and close the hole at the base of the thumb.

Right Hand

Cast on 36 sts *loosely*. You need to allow the ribbing to stretch.

Rounds 1 - 7: K1 P1 around

Rounds 8 - 9: K around

Round 10: K22 P1 Hold the yarn in front of your work. Pass the next 7 stitches over to the other needle (strand made). P1 K5.

Round 11: K22 P1 K7 P1 K5

Round 12: As round 10

Round 13: As round 11

Round 14: As round 10

Round 15: As round 11

Round 16: As round 10

Round 17: As round 11

Round 18: K22 P1 K3 Pick up the 4 strands from the bottom up and knit the next stitch. Pull the loop down through the 4 strands (Bow completed). K3 P1 K5

Round 19: K22 P1 K7 P1 K5 ✋

Repeat from ✋ to ✋ if you would like a longer length of glove. Each ✋ to ✋ repeat makes 1 bow motif.

Round 20: K1 M1 K1 M1 K20 P1 Hold the yarn in front of your work. Pass the next 7 stitches over to the other needle (strand made). P1 K5

Round 21: K to the P. P1 K7 P1 K5

Round 22: K to the P. P1 Hold the yarn in front of your work. Pass the next 7 stitches over to the other needle (strand made). P1 K5

Round 23: K1 M1 K3 M1 K20 P1 K7 P1 K5

Round 24: As round 22

Round 25: As round 21

Round 26: K1 M1 K5 M1 K20 P1 Hold the yarn in front of your work. Pass the next 7 stitches over to the other needle (strand made). P1 K5

Round 27: As round 21

Round 28: K to the P. P1 K3 Pick up the 4 strands from the bottom up and knit the next stitch. Pull the loop down through the 4 strands (Bow completed). K3 P1 K5

Round 29: K1 M1 K7 M1 K20 P1 K7 P1 K5

Round 30: As round 22

Round 31: As round 21

Round 32: K1 M1 K9 M1 K20 P1 Hold the yarn in front of your work. Pass the next 7 stitches over to the other needle (strand made). P1 K5

Round 33: As round 21

Round 34: As round 22

Round 35: K1 M1 K11 M1 K20 P1 K7 P1 K5

Round 36: As round 22

Round 37: As round 21

Round 38: K1 Pass next 13 stitches onto the stitch holder. K to the P. P1 K3. Pick up the 4 strands from the bottom up and knit the next stitch. Pull the loop down through the 4 strands (Bow completed). K3 P1 K5

Round 39: As round 21

Rounds 40 – 41: K around

Round 42: K2tog P1 K1 around. P1 in last stitch.

Round 43 – 46: K1 P1 around.

Cast off *loosely*.

Make Thumb

Pick up the 13 stitches from the stitch holder. Work 3 rounds even.

Cast off *loosely*.

Sew in the ends and close the hole at the base of the thumb.

Hints and Tips

I cast all the stitches on one needle when I start. Then I divide them up between the 3 needles. This helps to avoid the twisting you can sometimes get when casting on to each needle.

You don't need a stitch holder. Even a piece of yarn will work.

Spread the 7 passed stitches apart to allow for some slack in the strand. If you don't the bows will pucker. I usually spread them as far apart as they will go and stay in a relaxed position.

A quick note on making them longer into arm warmers. The green arm warmers repeat the bow section 4 *more* times than what is written. As it is written you get the short gloves with 3 bow motifs. Depending on the circumference of the arm you may need to add and cast on more stitches. This is where having the bows staying centred gets difficult. I can't really help you with that. It's a bunch of additional math, frustration and trial and error I really don't want to get into. Sorry.

Your gauge isn't overly important but best if it's at least close. Because the knitted mittens are are fingerless, they are very forgiving if they're a little small or large.

I prefer to use bamboo dpn. I find that it helps to prevent that line you get between needles when knitting in the round.

You will probably need to adjust the number of stitches you have on each needle. I usually make one split between 2 knit stitches *before* the purl at the start of the bow motif. It gives more than 12 on one needle and less than 12 on the other, but it makes it easier to knit the bow and lessens the chances of dropping or adding a stitch when switching between working needles.

When you are done making the bows, they may pull a bit weirdly on one side. Simply put your needle beneath the 4 strands and give a bit of a tug up away from the mitt on both sides. That is enough to straighten and even them out.

If you've gained a stitch, check to see that you haven't picked up a stitch between your needles. This is very easy to do and I even do it on occasion. When switching between needles the yarn will catch on the needle, not falling in behind again like it should. If you're a little distracted, you'll knit this new "stitch", gaining an extra stitch on the next round.

I haven't tried this, but changing to even smaller needles and thinner yarn (DK or 3 perhaps) can make even smaller child sizes. Let me know if you try this and what gauge and needles give the right sizes. You can leave your findings in the comment section.

Abbreviations:

K - Knit

P - Purl

Sts - stitches

K2tog - Knit 2 together

M1 – Make one (knit wise). Increase one stitch between the stitches. Pick up the yarn between the stitches. Twist it slightly and place it on your non-working needle. Knit the stitch. Watch this video on **How to M1 or Make 1** to see how.

Like all of my patterns you have my permission to sell and/or give away the physical items that you make using this pattern. You are NOT permitted to reprint this pattern in any form unless you have obtained my written permission to do so.

If you have any questions, please feel free to leave a comment or send me your questions at kweenbee_crafts@hotmail.ca.

Help Support My Work!

Follow me on Instagram, Facebook, Pinterest and YouTube. Every follow, subscribe, thumbs up, like, heart and share help increase my popularity on the web and get more viewers to my work. It costs you nothing but helps me sooooo much!

If you would like to help a little more, you can always become a Website Member to download and print over 50 patterns. Or you can support me by becoming a Patron on Patreon or you can make a single time donation at Buy Me a Coffee.

You can use any of these QR codes to find out more.

Website Member

Patreon

Buy Me a Coffee

More FREE knitting patterns on my website

I'm always creating new patterns and I post every one of them over on my website. It is an ever growing list so you might want to check out my page at **KweenBee.com**. I design new patterns as I get time. I aim to add a couple new ones each month so the list is always growing!

Below is a VERY small example of the other patterns that I have on the website.

Diamonds Discloth

Cozy Lace Up Slippers for Adults

Owl Bucket Hat

Winter Beanie Toque or Touque or Tuque with Vertical Stripes

Ultra Thick Slip-On Bootie Slippers

How to Knit a Beanie Hat – with OWLS!

Minimalist Round Toe Slippers

Autumn Leaf Half Gloves

Of course, none of the links will work. To make it even easier, you can take a photo of the QR code below with your phone or tablet. A link will pop up. Tap that link and it will take you right to the webpage to see all of the patterns including those above.

You can also do a search for the titles online if QR codes are something that you feel you are unable or don't want to use it.

When you are on your favourite search engine like Google, Bing, Yahoo, etc. Enter the term **Kweenbee,** the title or anything else you are looking for. It will pop up for you in the search results and be super-easy to find. There may be some ads at the top of the page, they'll be marked as ads, but scroll past those.

For example, enter it like this:

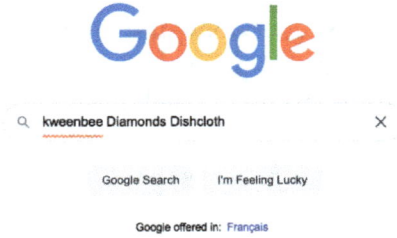

Your results will have my pattern at the very top...usually. Depending on the popularity of the pattern, you may get a link to Pinterest or Ravelry first. Don't worry! All of those options have links back to my original patterns, too!

Follow Me on Social Media

Take a photo with your phone or tablet of the QR codes below. A link will appear. Click the link to go straight to my social media page.

TikTok	**YouTube**	**Threads**
Facebook	**Instagram**	**Pinterest**
Patreon	**My Etsy Shop**	**Buy Me a Coffee**

Your Notes

*Velcro is a registered trademark.

www.ingramcontent.com/pod-product-compliance
Lightning Source LLC
Chambersburg PA
CBHW081006120626
46546CB00010B/3030